Whodunit Crime Puzzles

by Hy Conrad
illustrated by Tatjana Mai Wyss

Sterling Publishing Co., Inc.
New York

Dedicated to Steve Schaffer,
a true pioneer in the field.

Published by Sterling Publishing Company, Inc.
387 Park Avenue South, New York, N.Y. 10016
© 2002 by Hy Conrad and Tatjana Mai Wyss
Distributed in Canada by Sterling Publishing
C/o Canadian Manda Group, One Atlantic Avenue, Suite 105
Toronto, Ontario, Canada M6K 3E7
Distributed in Great Britain and Europe by Chris Lloyd
at Orca Book Services, Stanley House, Fleets Lane,
Poole BH15 3AJ, England
Distributed in Australia by Capricorn Link (Australia) Pty. Ltd.
P.O. Box 704, Windsor, NSW 2756 Australia

Sterling ISBN 0-8069-9796-6

CONTENTS

INTRODUCTION

No one knew where Sherman Oliver Holmes came from or how he'd gotten his money. One day, Capital City was just your run-of-the-mill metropolitan area. The next day, a short, rotund millionaire in a deerstalker cap began showing up at crime scenes, claiming to be the great-great-grandson of Sherlock Holmes and offering his expert opinion.

Sergeant Gunther Wilson of the Major Crimes Division was irritated by how often this eccentric little man with the southern drawl would appear within minutes of a grisly murder and stick his nose into official police business. What disturbed Wilson even more was the fact that this eccentric little man was nearly always right.

"The loony should be committed," Wilson had been heard to say on more than one occasion. "He always has some outlandish theory. I'd sign the commitment papers myself — if I didn't have a soft spot for him." But Wilson didn't have a soft spot. What he did have was a phenomenal record for solving cases, thanks in large part to his "loony" friend.

To his credit, Sherman wasn't much interested in taking credit. As far as the public was concerned, the Capital City police were simply doing a better job than ever before. So Sergeant Wilson decided to swallow his pride and befriend the exasperating, unique little gentleman who had nothing better to do than pop up like a fat rabbit and do the work of an entire detective squad.

THE MISSING MONET

Sherman Holmes didn't know how he did it; but he did, and on a regular basis. Sometimes he'd see a police cruiser and stop to see what was happening. Sometimes he'd follow the sound of a siren. More often than not, he would just be walking or driving around Capital City when a sixth sense would tell him to turn here or stop there.

It was this sixth sense for crime that brought him to the Hudson Office Building on a blustery March day. Sherman settled quietly into a chair in the lobby, patiently waiting for something to happen.

The first visitor to catch his eye was a bike messenger, arriving with a package-filled backpack and a long document tube. The messenger disappeared into an express elevator labeled 31st Floor. Five minutes later, the messenger reappeared and left the building, still carrying the tube but one package lighter.

Taking his place in the elevator was an elegantly attired man, an older gentleman, using a cane as he limped heavily on his left leg.

The gentleman reappeared in the lobby ten minutes later. On his exit from the elevator he nearly collided with a woman in a Gucci suit. The umbrella in her left hand became momentarily entangled with the cane in his right.

"Watch where you're going," she snapped.

"My apologies," he replied.

The man limped off and the woman pressed her button and fidgeted with her umbrella until the elevator door closed. Her visit lasted five minutes.

Sherman was beginning to think his crime-sensing instincts were flawed. Perhaps it was this nasty cold he was just getting over. Then a pair of police officers rushed into the lobby and took the same express elevator to the 31st floor. "It's about time they called in the police," Sherman said with satisfaction.

When they left the building a half hour later, Sherman followed them to the Baker Street Coffee Shop. He slipped into the booth behind theirs, quietly ordered an English muffin, and eavesdropped.

"What was a million-dollar painting doing in the reception area?" the older cop asked his partner. Sherman recognized him as Sergeant Gunther Wilson, an officer he'd chatted with at dozens of other crime scenes.

The 31st floor, it seems, contained the offices of the Hudson Company's top brass, and the furnishings in the reception area included a small Monet oil, about one foot square. Only three visitors had been alone there long enough to cut the painting out of its frame — a bike messenger delivering documents, the ne'er-do-well uncle of the company president wanting to borrow a few dollars, and the vice president's estranged wife, who had come to complain about her allowance. All three had visited the offices before and could have previously noticed the unguarded painting.

"Excuse me," Sherman said as he rose from his booth and ambled up to Officer Wilson and his partner.

Wilson saw the pudgy little man in his deerstalker cap and frock-coat and beamed. "Sherlock Holmes, I presume."

"That was my great-great-grandfather," Sherman answered politely. "But I did inherit a few of his modest powers. Would you like me to tell you who stole that painting?"

WHO STOLE THE PAINTING?
WHAT CLUE GAVE THE THIEF AWAY?

Solution on page 78.

A MAZE OF SUSPECTS

Sherman Holmes was out for a drive on a lonely country road. He saw the police car and the sign for the labyrinth maze at almost the same moment. "A labyrinth puzzle plus a crime," he chuckled, stepping on the brakes. "How lovely." He switched on his turn signal and pulled off into the parking lot.

The roadside attraction, "Queen Victoria's Maze," consisted of a ticket booth, a small, shabby office, and the maze itself, a seven-foot-high square of ill-kept hedges. Curious motorists were lured into paying three dollars apiece to get lost in the confusing pathways inside the hedges.

Sherman bypassed the empty ticket booth and wandered up a gravel path and into the maze itself. Two right turns brought him to a dead end — a dead end complete with a corpse. A highway patrolman was standing over the corpse of a casually dressed man, a knife stuck between his ribs. Three men and a woman faced the officer.

"My husband Kyle and I came into the maze and split up just for fun," the woman said between sobs. "After several minutes of wandering, I wound up outside at another entrance. I was going to try again. I called Kyle, to see how he was doing. That's when I heard it — some scuffling — like a fight. Then Kyle screamed."

"I heard the scream, too," said the tallest man. "I was on

a bench at the center of the maze. I didn't hear any scuffling, probably because the fountain there drowned it out. I'm Bill McQuire. I hurried out of the maze and found Mrs. Turner. The two of us went back in and discovered the body together."

"I'm the owner," said a short, disheveled man. "Paul Moran. These people were the only three customers in there. After taking the Turners' money at the ticket booth, I went into the office. Abe, my electrician, was rewiring the system. I switched off the main fuse box for him. Then I walked around picking up trash. Abe was still working when I heard a man's scream."

Abe, the electrician, was the last to speak. "What Paul said is true. I was in a crawl space under the office the whole time, doing the wiring. I didn't see anything or hear anyone until the scream."

The officer bent down to examine the body. "No wallet. Maybe it was a botched robbery. But we'll have to wait for the experts."

"I'm an expert," came a voice from behind. They turned around to find a short, owlish man with a briar pipe

between his teeth. "Sherman Holmes, at your service. The solution is elementary, if you'd care to listen."

WHO KILLED KYLE TURNER?
HOW DID SHERMAN DEDUCE THE TRUTH?

Solution on page 79.

BUS STATION BOMBER

"Where have you been?" Sergeant Wilson stepped around the burned and mangled debris of what had been the rear wall of the Capital City bus terminal. "I thought you must be sick."

Gunther Wilson was secretly dependent on Sherman Holmes's habit of showing up uninvited at crime scenes. He certainly wasn't used to waiting three hours for the odd, pudgy millionaire to make an appearance.

"Sorry, old man." Sherman sniffled. "I haven't been myself. Spring allergies."

Wilson pointed to a four-man squad arranging charred bits of metal on a white sheet. "The bomb was in a locker. It went off at three P.M. There were a few injuries, but nothing serious. The mechanism was an old wind-up clock wired to two sticks of dynamite. It was triggered by the alarm mechanism hitting the '3'."

"Do you have a motive?"

"Not a clue. My guess is he did it for the thrill, like some of the sick arsonists we've dealt with lately."

"Let's hope we catch him before he tries again." Sherman glanced around the terminal. "Did anyone see who used the locker?"

"I got in touch with the night clerk." Wilson waved over a slight, sleepy-looking man. "Mr. Pollard, tell my associate what you saw."

"Certainly." Andy Pollard adjusted his thick eyeglasses and cleared his throat. "Last night as I was coming in to work, around two A.M., I saw this cabdriver parking out front. He walked in with a red travel bag and put it in that locker."

Wilson waved again and two more men crossed to join them. "We checked with the cab companies. Only two taxis were in the area around two A.M. Unfortunately, Mr. Pollard can't identify the driver."

"I remember the red bag," Pollard apologized, "but not the guy's face."

The first driver was a tall, fair-haired lad, barely out of high school.

"I've been driving for about a month," he explained. "I picked up a passenger at the airport and dropped her off at the hotel on the corner. That was around two. Then I filled up at the gas station on Highland and ended my shift. If this guy says I came in here, he's lying. I haven't been in a bus station in years."

The second driver was around the same height but middle-aged and with a pronounced gut hanging over his belt. "I dropped off a fare in front of the terminal," he told them. "My fare said he'd left his car in the parking lot earlier in the day and had to pick it up. That was a few minutes after two.

"Then my dispatcher sent me to a bar on Fifth to pick up a drunk. No one was there. A man waved me down and I took him to an all-night diner on Swann Street. It's all in my log book if you don't believe me."

One of the members of the bomb squad was standing by, waiting for a chance to speak. "Excuse me, Sarge," he said. "The container was a red bag, just like the witness said. A red leather satchel."

"Thanks," Wilson said, then turned to Sherman and shrugged. "Not much to go on, huh?"

"Just enough to give us the bomber," Sherman purred. "I can't tell you why he did it, but I can certainly tell you who."

WHO BOMBED THE BUS STATION?
WHAT FACT CLUED SHERMAN IN?

Solution on page 79.

THE POSTMAN RINGS ONCE

Sergeant Wilson found the letter and envelope torn up and crammed into the bottom of a wastebasket. Reassembling it while wearing plastic gloves proved difficult.

"It's from Henry Liggit's lawyer," he finally said, looking up from the jigsaw-like puzzle. "It outlines Mr. Liggit's proposed new will, disinheriting his three nephews and leaving everything to charity."

Sherman stood behind the sergeant, peering over his shoulder. "What do you think?" Wilson asked him.

"Hmm. It doesn't take a Sherman Holmes," said Sherman Holmes, "to suspect that Mr. Liggit's suicide wasn't really a suicide."

"My thoughts exactly," the officer agreed.

Sherman and the sergeant were in Henry Liggit's library, just yards from where the millionaire lay slumped in his chair with a gun in his hand and a hole in his head.

"Our first job, my dear Wilson, will be determining which devoted nephew opened Liggit's mail and discovered the threat to his inheritance." With that, Sherman led the way into the front hall where the nervous nephews stood waiting.

All three nephews lived in the Liggit house; all three had been at home at the time of the shot. None, or so they swore, had the least idea Uncle Henry had been about to cut them out of his will.

"Uncle Henry had been depressed," said Nigel, the eldest, in mournful tones. He was sipping a martini and Sherman suspected it wasn't his first of the day. "I spent all afternoon at home. About three P.M. I walked into the front hall. I was checking the mail on that side table when I heard the gunshot."

Sherman observed a few pieces of mail on the table. "When did the mail arrive, my good fellows?"

Gerald, the youngest nephew, raised his hand. "When I got home around 2:30, the mail was already on the hall floor. I walked right across it before noticing. I picked it up and put it on the hall table."

"Did you check through it?"

Gerald nodded. "Yes, but there was nothing for me. I went straight out to the garden and sat by the pool. I, too, heard the gunshot. Around three, as Nigel said."

"I looked through the mail," volunteered the middle nephew, Thomas. "I'd just got home from a trip. I put my bags down in the hall, sorted through, and found a letter for me. I put it in my pocket, then went up to my room."

"What time was this?"

"Ten minutes to three, or thereabouts. I was unpacking when I heard the shot."

"Is the letter still in your pocket?"

With some hesitation, Thomas reached into his jacket and produced the unopened envelope. Sherman noticed a faint shoe print, a water ring, and a curious return address. "It's from a bill collector," Thomas confessed. "I've got a cash flow problem."

"Can anyone verify your arrival at the house at 2:50?"

"I can," said Gerald. "You can see the driveway from poolside. Thomas's car pulled in about ten minutes before poor Uncle killed himself."

"Yes," said Sherman. "We'll talk about suicide in a minute. Did any of you notice a letter addressed to your uncle from his lawyer?"

The nephews all shook their heads.

"Then that settles it," said Sherman. "One of you is lying. One of you knew about your uncle's plans to change his will and killed him before he could do it."

"I don't know what you're talking about," said Nigel.

"Join the club," laughed Sergeant Wilson. "I don't know what he's talking about half the time, either. But he's usually right."

WHO KILLED HENRY LIGGIT?
WHAT PROOF DOES SHERMAN HAVE?

Solution on page 80.

FOUL BALL BURGLARY

Sherman Holmes sat on a park bench, watching as the neighborhood boys played a pick-up game of baseball. "I should retrieve my great-great-grandfather's bat and teach those lads the art of cricket," the amateur detective thought, then realized he didn't know how to play it himself.

"Oh, well," he sighed. "The lads are awfully close to those houses." And that, of course, was the exact moment when the batter hit a long fly in just that direction. Glass shattered and a home alarm began to wail.

The left fielder, a boy called Jake, went after the ball. He

scrambled up a high wooden fence and straddled the top, gazing at the house and yard below. "The ball broke a window, all right," he shouted back to the others. Then his eyes widened. "Hey — you better call the police. I think there's been a robbery."

The game broke up immediately. Jake lowered himself into the backyard while the other boys circled around to the front of the house and awaited the police.

Jake unlocked the door from inside and let the officers in. Sherman sneaked in right behind. The rotund little Southerner was safely ensconced behind a potted palm when a man and a woman drove up in separate cars.

The newcomers joined the police inside. Sherman edged his potted palm into a good viewing position and managed to piece together the essentials.

The newcomers were brother and sister, Larry and Laura Conners. The house had belonged to their late father, who

kept his coin collection on display on a table by the rear garden window. This was what Jake must have seen from the fence. The heavy table lay on its side, not far from the wayward baseball. Remnants of the broken window were everywhere. A patrolman walked across the fallen table-cloth and Sherman could hear the muted crunch of glass under the white linen.

The Conners both had keys and both knew the alarm code. They had been here together just this morning, arguing about the coins.

"Laura must've come back and stolen them," snarled Larry. "Then she overturned the table in some pathetic attempt to blame it on a burglar. I was at home, ten miles from here, washing my car. My neighbors saw me. I was there right up until you called me."

Laura glared at her brother. "I was at home, too, eight miles in the other direction. I was on the phone with Aunt Doreen and doing my laundry. You can check with her if you want to."

Sherman wanted to jump out from behind the palm and instantly solve the case. But that might seem a little odd. So he restrained himself and waited until the officers were leaving.

WHO STOLE THE COINS?
WHAT CLUE POINTS TO THE THIEF?

Solution on page 81.

THE UNSAFE SAFE HOUSE

For all the help Sherman Holmes provided the police, he received little if any recognition. In fact, the officers he helped the most were often the first to make fun of his quirky personality. "They don't want people thinking some amateur is solving their cases," Sherman would say with a generous shrug. "I just wish I didn't have to sneak around eavesdropping all the time."

One of Sherman's most extreme eavesdropping cases involved hiding behind a coatrack for over an hour. On that day, his instincts for crime led him beyond a yellow-tape barricade and into the front hall of a police safe house, a normal-looking home in a modest, pleasant-looking row house in which a mob witness had just been murdered.

From behind the safety of the coats, Sherman watched as a nervous rookie stood over the body of the strangled man. A minute later, Captain Loeb strode in, his baggy suit flapping in the breeze.

"I was here protecting the witness," stammered the rookie. "Then I got a call from your office, ordering me back to the station. I left him alone. By the time I figured out the call was a fake and rushed back here, Frankie was dead."

The captain remained calm. "Who all has keys to the front door?"

"Just me," answered the rookie. "The door locked automatically behind me. I told Frankie not to open up to anyone."

Captain Loeb examined the body. "Strangled from behind, meaning he probably trusted his assailant. Who would Frankie open the door for? Let's get them in here."

The first suspect to be brought in was Lou, the victim's brother-in-law. "Frankie sneaked a telephone call to me last night at work," Lou said, staring down at the corpse. "I'm a phone company operator. Frankie didn't tell me where he was. My wife is going to go nuts when she hears."

The second suspect was Barry Aiello, the secret mob

informant who had talked Frankie into testifying. "I feel like I'm responsible," he sighed. "The mob was using all their contacts to find him." Barry bent down and examined the welts around the victim's neck. "Looks like a belt was used. Poor Frankie shouldn't have turned his back."

Captain Loeb had them both taken in for questioning, then crossed to the rack and grabbed his trench coat. "The commissioner's gonna have my head, but I suppose I gotta call him." Loeb had just pulled a notepad from his coat pocket when he saw a face staring out from behind Frankie's leather jacket. "Who in blazes are you?"

"Hi!" Sherman was so nervous, he momentarily forgot his English accent. "I'm so sorry. I know I'm trespassing, but..." He could think of only one way to redeem himself, and that was to hand them Frankie's killer.

WHO KILLED FRANKIE?
WHAT TIPPED SHERMAN OFF?

Solution on page 82.

THE CRYSTAL VANISHES

Luther brought a new pot of coffee into the dining room and began refreshing everyone's cup. "Agatha, is that the crystal ball you were telling us about?"

"Isn't it gorgeous!" The young woman in the flowing robe held it up for all to see, a round piece of cut crystal, not much larger than a baseball. "The salesman guaranteed me that it once belonged to Morgan LeFay. And this wasn't her everyday crystal either. It was her special one." Agatha passed the ball to Sherman Holmes.

"It's blooming lovely," Sherman said, managing to keep a straight face. He enjoyed his weekly dinners with Luther, Agatha, and Grimelda. The warlock and two witches might seem a little extreme to Sherman's other friends, but they were full of life and always interesting. And they accepted without question Sherman's own idiosyncrasies.

All three examined the ball, then watched as Agatha returned it to the red velvet box. "They say it has a mind of its own. If the crystal doesn't like its current owner, it will find a new one. We get along swimmingly, I'm glad to say."

The evening was almost over. Agatha helped Luther, the host, clear the dining room table, while Grimelda went to the bathroom and Sherman browsed through Luther's library. When he returned to the living room, Grimelda was adjusting her shawl and checking her makeup in the mirror over the mantle. She had always been the most attractive witch in the coven. Sherman had heard from Luther that there was some tension between her and the younger, newer arrival, Agatha.

"Next week at my abode," Sherman reminded her.

Grimelda seemed startled. "Oh, that's right. We're going to help you contact Dr. Watson. We never had much luck contacting your great-great-grandfather, did we?"

"We'll have to keep trying. Luther!" he shouted to the next room. "A scrumptious dinner." Then he saw the velvet box on the sideboard beside the full pot of coffee. "Agatha, don't forget your crystal." Sherman picked up the box and could instantly tell it was too light.

"It's gone," Agatha cried when she discovered the empty box. "Morgan's crystal has left me. I feel so rejected!"

"Oh, that's too bad," Grimelda commiserated. Luther agreed. The three witches seemed quite willing to accept the crystal's disappearance as a natural phenomenon. But Sherman knew better.

WHO TOOK THE CRYSTAL BALL?
WHERE IS IT HIDDEN?

Solution on page 82.

THE POINTING CORPSE

When the detective business was slow, the great Sherlock Holmes had spent the long, empty hours playing the violin. Sherman Holmes did the same, but with less soothing results. "Maybe I should take lessons," he would think as he sawed back and forth across the strings. When things got really slow, Sherman switched on one of his police band radios.

After two boring days of drizzle and inactivity, the detective intercepted a call reporting a murder victim found in a car. Sherman happened to be driving his classic Bentley at the time and made a quick turn up High Canyon Road.

He arrived to find Gunther Wilson standing between his patrol car and a white sedan parked beside a panoramic

view. The sergeant actually looked glad to see him. "I'm a little out of my depth on this one," he said. "It's a celebrity, Mervin Hightower. Shot at close range. I'm waiting for forensics and a tow truck. On top of being murdered, his car battery's dead."

The whole city knew Mervin Hightower, a newspaper columnist who specialized in scandalous exposés. Sherman walked around to the driver's side. An arm extended out the partially open window, propped up on the glass edge. The hand was made into a fist, except for the index finger, which was straight and firm with rigor mortis.

"He appears to be pointing," Sherman deduced. "How long has the fellow been dead?"

"What do I look like, a clock? The forensics boys will narrow it down. I saw the car and stopped to see if he needed help, which he doesn't. I recognized him, even with the blood."

Sherman looked in to see the columnist's familiar face contorted and frozen in agony. "I presume the man survived for a minute after the attack. What do you think he was pointing at, old bean? Something that could identify his killer?" Sherman lined up his eyes along the extended arm. "What story was he working on?"

Wilson pulled a newspaper from his back pocket. "Here. In today's column, he says he's going to expose some embezzlement from the City Charity Board."

"There are only three people on the Charity Board," Sherman said, checking the column for their names. "Marilyn Lake, Arthur Curtis, and Tony Pine." Then he examined the view: a glistening lake, a neon sign for Curtis Furniture and a majestic grove of evergreens. "Zounds!"

"Zounds is right. If Mervin was trying to point out his killer, he did a lousy job."

"Not necessarily." Sherman was thinking. "I think he did just fine."

WHO KILLED MERVIN HIGHTOWER?
HOW DID SHERMAN KNOW?

Solution on page 83.

BELL, BOOKE, OR KENDAL?

"My regrets, Wilson. I have no idea who killed him."

"What?" Sergeant Wilson thought he would never hear Sherman Holmes say those words. He wasn't too happy about it, either. "Okay, okay, calm down." Wilson sounded close to panic himself. "Mr. Boren, maybe you should review the facts."

Sherman and the sergeant were in the downtown offices of Boren Technologies, a designer of handheld computers. Arvin Boren sat at his desk, eyeing the professional detective and the eccentric amateur. "Someone's been stealing our designs. My vice president, Don Silver, and I kept the problem secret. And we narrowed the suspects down to three." He pointed out the window of his private office to where a skinny kid in shirtsleeves was stuffing yellow envelopes into a mail slot.

"That's Wally Bell, an intern from City College. He does a lot of our copying and binding, so he has access to our priority documents. The heavyset guy sitting outside my office, that's Solly Booke, my assistant. He's sending his son to private school. I don't know where he gets the money.

"The third possibility is Inez Kendal." A young woman in a tasteful, expensive suit was tacking a newspaper article to a bulletin board right next to the elevators. "Inez is director of public relations. She has the most contact with our competitors."

Sherman nodded. "Was it Mr. Silver's idea to try to trap the traitor?"

"I'm afraid so," Boren sighed. "We're developing a new version of our Wrist 2002. Don left the plans lying conspicuously on his desk. The thief never took originals, only copies. Don planned to hide in the copy room and catch the guy. Only the guy must have caught him."

Sergeant Wilson took over the narrative. "Silver was killed in the copy room by a blow to the head. Mr. Boren and an associate found the body almost immediately. All three suspects were immediately sequestered and their possessions searched. We haven't been able to locate the plans."

Sherman took the sergeant across to the window but didn't lower his voice. "The thief couldn't afford to be caught with them. My guess is the plans got thrown down that mail slot. It's the only place they could be."

Five minutes later, Sergeant Wilson persuaded a maintenance man to open the ground-floor mail chute. There the plans were, nestled right on top of a layer of yellow envelopes. "Just as I thought," Sherman said, turning to Wilson. "Now I know the killer."

WHO KILLED DON SILVER?
HOW DID SHERMAN KNOW?

Solution on page 83.

THE WAYWARD WILL

Sherman Holmes signed his name to the will and then watched as Harmon Grove signed as the other witness. "Thanks for dropping over — again," the congenial lawyer said as he slipped the will into his briefcase. "The Fielding kids can't be witnesses because they inherit."

"Not a problem," Sherman replied. This was the fourth time he had been asked over to witness a new version of Jacob Fielding's will. "You get better now, Jake," Sherman said to the frail man propped up in bed. Jacob nodded weakly and closed his eyes.

Sherman and the lawyer walked out into the hall. "This may be the old man's last will," Harmon whispered. "I don't expect he'll last the night." Solemn-faced, Anna passed them and entered the sick room.

There were three Fielding children. As their next-door neighbor, Sherman knew them well — Anna, the nurse; Brock, now a surgeon at a local hospital; and Keith, fresh out of college. All three had moved back into the family home during their father's long, difficult illness.

Harmon deposited his briefcase on the dining room table, and walked Sherman to the door. As they entered the foyer, Anna appeared at the top of the stairs. "Mr. Grove, I think...I think he's dead."

The two men joined the Fielding children who had already gathered in the dead man's bedroom. Brock checked for vital signs, then gently pulled the sheet over his father's face.

Half an hour later, as the people from the funeral home were removing the body, Sherman and Harmon once more crossed through the dining room. Harmon saw his briefcase and eyed it curiously. "It's been moved," he said, then opened the leather lid. "The new will. It's gone!"

Sherman and the lawyer backtracked their movements through the bedroom, dining room, and hall, hoping to find the will somehow mislaid. Finally they had no choice but to assemble the bereaved children and treat them as suspects.

"I went downstairs once after he died," Anna claimed. "To get the number for the funeral home. I called them from the kitchen. I didn't go into the dining room, and I certainly didn't touch your briefcase."

"I went downstairs to let the funeral people in," Dr. Brock Fielding said. "I saw the briefcase but didn't touch it. I didn't even know the will was in there."

Keith sighed. "Well, I didn't go downstairs at all. After

Brock declared father dead, I returned to my room to call some relatives. What do we do if we can't find the will?"

"We'll have to use his last will," Harmon explained. "It's almost exactly the same. You know how eccentric he was. All three of you still get substantial bequests. He left me the same token gift. Plus small amounts go to servants and employees."

"I can find the new will," Sherman said softly. The others all turned, a little surprised to find him still in the room. "I think I know where to look."

WHERE IS THE NEW WILL?
HOW DID SHERMAN KNOW?

Solution on page 84.

THE DOC'S LAST LUNCH

Sergeant Wilson hated stakeouts. Here he was, stuck alone in a first-floor apartment, photographing the comings and goings at the home of a suspected hit man across the street. And it was a beautiful day outside, which just made things worse.

Wilson heard the door to his own apartment building close and glanced outside to see Dr. Weber's regular Tuesday patient leaving. 11:58, he noted on his watch. Time for the elderly psychiatrist to watch his half-hour game show, and then make himself lunch. When he concentrated, Wilson could hear the TV upstairs in the doctor's living room.

At 12:35, the whistle of a teakettle announced the doctor's lunch preparations. Three minutes later, the kettle was still whistling furiously. Wilson abandoned his stakeout and hurried one flight up to see if anything was wrong.

When his knocking produced no response, Wilson walked into the unlocked apartment. The doctor lay on the kitchen floor. A fruit knife lay in his right hand. A bloody steak knife lay imbedded in his back.

Wilson did his own whistling. "Wow."

"Wow is correct, dear fellow."

The sergeant turned to find Sherman Holmes standing behind him in the doorway. "This murder just happened,"

Wilson gasped. "How do you do it? You're like a vulture."

"Thanks awfully," Sherman said and quickly perused the scene. The noisy teakettle sat on a low flame. On a cutting board were an open can of tuna and a sliced apple, its flesh already turned brown. The TV was on in the background. "Someone interrupted his lunch."

"That much seems clear," Wilson said. "There are two other tenants in this building who stay home during the day. Let's talk to them."

Sammy Cole, on the third floor, answered the door in his underwear. "I work nights," he said with a yawn. "I got home around 11 A.M., had a little breakfast, and went to bed." Sherman looked through to Cole's kitchen and saw a half-filled carafe sitting in the automatic coffee maker. "The floors are thick," Sammy added. "I didn't hear a thing."

Glenda Gould lived across the hall from Sammy and seemed unnerved by Dr. Weber's death. "He was my psychiatrist. I told him to get better security. With all the nut cases he treats, this sort of attack was inevitable." She twisted the ring on her finger, revealing a raw patch of skin underneath. "I'll need to find another doctor."

Wilson walked back down to the crime-scene apartment with Holmes. "Naturally I know who did it," Sherman said in his unique, infuriating way. "I just need to check one thing."

WHO IS SHERMAN'S SUSPECT?
WHAT WAS THE VITAL CLUE?

Solution on page 85.

A HALLOWEEN HOMICIDE

Sherman loved Halloween. It gave him a chance to dress up as Sherlock Holmes and still seem normal. The pudgy detective was in his usual costume, escorting a squadron of children down Elm Street, when he noticed a crowd gathering in front of old Miss Cleghorn's house. "She must be up to her usual," chortled Sherman. "Putting on some horrific mask and scaring the kids at the door."

Miss Cleghorn was indeed scaring the kids, but not intentionally. Inside the open door, Sherman could see her frail body lying in the entry hall, wearing a monster mask, her head surrounded by blood. A plastic bowl lay nearby, its contents of wrapped candy strewn everywhere.

Sergeant Wilson stood beside the body. He glanced over

at the man with the calabash pipe and deerstalker cap. "Is that a costume, Holmes? With you it's hard to tell."

"What happened, my respectable partner in crime?"

"It's an accident. It took us a while to reconstruct what happened." Wilson pointed up to where a strand of large pearls lay centered at the top of the steps. "She was upstairs when the first trick-or-treaters rang the bell. She put on the mask and grabbed the bowl. She must have slipped on the pearls and tumbled down the stairs."

Two cars pulled up at the curb, one behind the other. Sherman recognized Miss Cleghorn's niece and nephew, Emma and Bobby, as they got out of the cars and approached the front door, both dressed for a night out and seemingly unaware of the tragedy.

"Aunt Rita," Bobby gasped.

"Your aunt had an accident," Sergeant Wilson told them. "She's dead. The kids had been coming up to the door for half an hour or so and getting no answer. One of them finally looked through the window and saw her."

Bobby noticed the spilled candy and the mask. "What's she doing wearing a mask?"

"She was obviously doing her Halloween thing," Emma said.

"She promised she wouldn't this year. We were taking her out to dinner."

"Well, obviously she changed her mind," Emma said, shaking her head. "I don't know how many times I told her not to wear a mask on the stairs."

"When did you last see your aunt?" asked Sherman.

Bobby stared at the rather overage trick-or-treater. "Uh, I dropped by this morning. My daughter left her skateboard here. Aunt Rita made me coffee and we chatted."

Sergeant Wilson grabbed Sherman by the collar and dragged him aside. "Don't try to make this a murder. The neighbors say there were no visitors since this morning."

"Someone could have driven up the back alley and come in that way," argued Sherman. "Believe me, friend, this was murder."

WHY COULDN'T IT HAVE BEEN ACCIDENTAL?
WHOM DOES SHERMAN SUSPECT AND WHY?

Solution on page 85.

THE COMMERCIAL
BREAK BREAK-IN

An inch of snow fell that evening, turning to a crusty sleet that hardened and made everything beautiful and treacherous. When the skies cleared, Sherman went for a stroll.

"What ho, Trent! A quiet night, eh?" Sherman waved to the uniformed guard hired to patrol the neighborhood.

"A little too quiet." Tom Trent was naturally suspicious and pessimistic, good traits for a neighborhood security guard. At the moment, he was scanning his flashlight beam across the suburban landscape. "Uh-oh." His light stopped on the side of the Warner family's home.

Sherman saw what he meant. The ladder that Bill Warner had used last fall to paint the house was now propped up against it, leading up to a second-story window. The flashlight beam scanned the rest of the house. Lights were on downstairs but not upstairs. The family had undoubtedly come home before the snowfall, since there were no footprints going up the walkway. But there were other footprints, a single set leading to the dry space under the eaves where the ladder was usually stored. The same prints led to where the ladder now stood, then retreated back to the sidewalk.

Trent checked out the ladder, stepping on the first rung and causing the wooden feet to crunch into the hardened snow. Without a word, the guard crossed to the front door,

drew his revolver, and knocked. Sherman followed.

Amelia Warner answered the door. "Tom. Sherman. What's wrong?"

"Possible break-in," Trent replied, then asked a few questions. Amelia, Bill, and Frank, a visiting friend, had been home for about three hours. For the past hour, no one had gone upstairs. And no one had propped the ladder up against the house.

"Stay here," Trent ordered everyone. Then he tiptoed up the stairs and vanished around a corner. Two minutes later, he called out. "It's all clear. Come on up."

When Sherman, the Warners, and their houseguest entered the master bedroom, they found the remains of a robbery. Drawers lay open; closets were in shambles. Bill and Amelia raced to check their valuables. Bill's wallet was gone. So were the rings and earrings from Amelia's jewelry box.

No one, it seems, had heard anything. "We were watching TV," Bill Warner said. "I went down to the basement during a commercial. I was looking for an old school yearbook to show Frank. I couldn't find it."

"I went to the kitchen for snacks and drinks," Amelia reported. "I think I went twice, during two commercial breaks."

"And I used the bathroom," said Frank. "Someone must have noticed the lights off upstairs and seen the ladder and just taken the opportunity. It wouldn't take long to grab the valuables. People always neglect to lock upstairs windows."

Amelia turned to Sherman. "You're always bragging about your great-great-grandfather. Why don't you put that genetic brilliance to a little use?"

WHO BURGLED THE BEDROOM?
HOW DID SHERMAN SOLVE THE CASE?

Solution on page 86.

AN ALARMING JEWEL HEIST

"Maybe now you'll stop bugging me," Zach Alban said as Sherman walked into his friend's shop. "See? I got that alarm system you recommended, wired straight to the police station."

"It's about time," Sherman replied. Alban Jewelers had just expanded its business and finally had some jewels worth stealing.

"Mr. Alban, I'm leaving now." Ricky Mayfield had

finished clearing out the window displays, placing the felts of precious stones into their locked drawers for the night. The door buzzed as the young assistant raced out to catch his bus.

Melanie, Alban's second in command, was putting on her jacket and looking at the newly installed alarm panel. "Are you sure you don't want to give me the code, Zach? That way you won't always have to be here to open and close."

"Not right now. Maybe in a few days when I get more used to it."

"Whatever," Melanie said. A rumbling from the street announced the arrival of her boyfriend's motorcycle. "See you tomorrow." And she was quickly out the door, hopping onto the back of a Harley-Davidson.

Zach led the way into the back office, eager to show his friend the entire system. "Once I set the code, any broken window or open door will trigger the alarm. Twenty seconds, that's all the time I have to disarm it. Sam, why don't you go home, too?"

Sam Wells switched off the computer and wished his boss a good night. Seconds later they heard the front door buzz, signaling the last employee's departure. "Want to help me close up?" Zach asked Sherman. "I don't want to make a mistake. After your first false alarm, they start charging you a fine."

Sherman and Zach followed the instructions to the letter, then went down the block to Gil's Tavern. When they left an hour later, Sherman noticed a police patrol car parked in front of Alban Jewelers.

"Break-in and burglary," an officer informed the devastated storeowner. "The back alley window was smashed. We responded within two minutes. But the alley was empty and the crooks were already gone."

Sherman was surprised by the thoroughness of the burglary. The jewel drawers had been chiseled open and stripped of their contents. The display cases had also been broken into and ransacked, glass shards littering the hardwood floor.

"So much for my brand new alarm system," Zach said almost accusingly.

"Not so fast," Sherman said. "If it weren't for the alarm system I wouldn't know who the burglar is."

WHO ROBBED THE SHOP?
HOW DID SHERMAN KNOW?

Solution on page 87.

ALL IN THE FAMILY

Sergeant Wilson enjoyed an occasional breakfast with Sherman at the Baker Street Coffee Shop. What he didn't enjoy were the homicide calls that so often came right in the middle of the meal. He was just finishing his Belgian waffle with fruit when this morning's call took him to Gleason & Son Insurance, located on a lonely stretch of highway. As usual, Sherman tagged along.

A uniformed officer met them in the parking lot. "The victim is Gary Lovett," the officer told them. "A Gleason & Son employee. That's Neal Gleason and his sister, Patty Lovett. She's the victim's widow." He was pointing to an anxious-looking duo, both in their late twenties. "Mr. Gleason discovered the body at about 8:30 A.M."

Neal Gleason stepped forward. His statement sounded rehearsed. "When I pulled into the parking lot, I saw Gary's car. Gary is often here early, though he's always gone before noon. If Gary wasn't Patty's husband, Dad would've fired him long ago. The front door was open. Right inside the door I saw him, like that."

Wilson examined the body in the doorway. The man's head was a bloody mess, and it took the sergeant a while to realize that the rifle now bagged as evidence had been used as a blunt instrument, its wooden stock having been slammed into his head like a baseball bat. The body was cold and rigor mortis had already come and gone.

"That's my husband's rifle," volunteered the widow. "He kept it here at the office. Last night at home, Gary got this phone call. He said he had to go the office and that I should just go to bed. I thought he might be going to see another woman. This morning when I woke up he was still gone. So I went to find him. I must have arrived here just a minute after my brother did."

"I think we should probably call Dad," Neal said.

That call wouldn't be necessary, for at that exact moment, George Gleason was pulling into the parking lot. The burly insurance broker eased himself out of his Cadillac and wordlessly took in the scene, the body, the bagged rifle, and his two children.

Patty ran up to him. "Someone murdered Gary," she moaned. "The police suspect us, Neal and me."

Gleason hugged his daughter, exchanged glances with his

son, then turned to face Sergeant Wilson. "I killed him," he said softly and simply. "I met him here last night and shot him, right in the head. My kids had nothing to do with it."

As the uniform took Gleason's statement, Wilson stepped off to the side with Sherman. "You don't have to tell me," Wilson whispered. "I picked up on the clue, too."

"Perhaps, old man," Sherman said with a smile. "But did you pick up on the right clue?"

WHO KILLED GARY LOVETT?
WHAT CLUE POINTS TO THE KILLER?

Solution on page 87.

THE LOST ETRUSCAN FIND

Sergeant Gunther Wilson rolled the library ladder over the shards of glass and water, then climbed to the top rung. "This skylight must be how the thief got in," he said, pointing to the smashed skylight and the rope dangling down into the room from a crossbeam. "Forensics can use this ladder to dust for prints."

"There won't be any prints," said a familiar, high-pitched voice. The sergeant gazed down to see Sherman Holmes standing below him in the university's research library.

"What're you doing here?" Wilson barked.

"The victim asked me to help out."

Sherman, it turned out, was a friend of Professor Plotny, the man who had acquired the small Etruscan statue that had just been stolen.

"I spent a fortune of my own money on that statuette." The burly professor wrung his hands. "I left it on the center table when I exited the building last night. I locked the door. But, of course, anyone up on the roof could have looked in and seen it."

Sergeant Wilson shook his head. "No thief goes around rooftops with a rope, just hoping someone left valuables on a table. It had to be someone who knew the statuette and knew your rather careless habits."

A small, wiry man stepped forward, brandishing an

authentic English accent Sherman would have killed for. "Next to no one knew about the statue, officer. I'm Donald Westbank, an Etruscan expert. I arrived yesterday from London. Dr. Plotny and I examined the statue together and, frankly, I was thrilled. What a find! I was a little jet-lagged, so I left the library around six, just in time for that little storm you had. I took a cab to the hotel and ordered from room service. When I got here this morning, I found Gina, the professor's assistant, unlocking the doors."

Gina, an athletic-looking graduate student, came forward with her story. "I left Professor Plotny and Mr. Westbank here yesterday at 5:30 P.M. My dorm room is just around the block. I did some studying until seven, when the rain stopped. Then I joined a friend at the Cathay Café for Chinese food. I got back to my room around 8:30."

"And your dorm building is on the other side of this block?" Wilson asked. "Are the roofs all connected?"

"How would I know if the roofs are connected?" she said. "And I resent your implication."

"So do I," the professor added. "It must have been an outsider. If you want to know my whereabouts...I left the library around 7:15 to drive to my brother's for a birthday party. I spent the night with his family and was the last one to get back here this morning."

Sergeant Wilson took Sherman Holmes aside. "I'm in the dark," he whispered. "But I know you've got it all figured out."

"As a matter of fact, no," Sherman lied. "I haven't a clue."

WHO STOLE THE STATUE?
WHAT CLUE POINTS TO THE THIEF?

Solution on page 88.

BLUE CARBUNCLE, THE SEQUEL

Once a year, on his birthday, Sherman Holmes threw a dinner party. The cream of Capital City's eccentrics would gather in his large, comfortable home, along with neighbors and other friends, to eat and drink and laugh.

At this year's celebration, after everyone else had left, Sherman and his three last guests sat over brandies in his living room, discussing the one inexhaustible topic, the Sherlock Holmes mysteries.

"What exactly is a carbuncle?" Dora Treat asked. Someone had brought up "The Adventure of the Blue Carbuncle," and the nurse practitioner was curious. "The only carbuncle I know is a skin infection, like a boil."

Buddy Johnson, a jeweler, chuckled. "It's a gemstone, a deep red garnet. Carbuncles are never blue. That was a figment of Conan Doyle's imagination."

Sherman puckered his round face into a frown. "But there is a blue carbuncle. Dr. Watson wouldn't lie about a thing like that."

"Yes, of course," Sam Pickering stammered. Their host seemed so rational in every other respect, it was easy to forget his fixation. "What Buddy meant was there are no other known blue carbuncles, just that one."

"Exactly," Sherman said. "That's why it was so expensive. Would you all like to see it?"

His guests were flabbergasted. "You mean you actually own the blue carbuncle?" asked Sam. "The one from the story?" The newspaper reporter had already done two articles about the unconventional millionaire and he could sense a third one in the making.

"The gem dealer assured me it's the real thing. Come into the library and I'll show you."

The room they walked into looked more like a junk room than a library, with first editions strewn on the chairs along with stacks of old papers and magazines. Sherman took three small boxes down from a shelf. He rummaged through the blue one, flipped through the red one, and finally found what he wanted in the green box.

"Here it is."

From among a pile of receipts and marbles, he pulled out a blue gem, about the size of a pea. Buddy Johnson pulled a jeweler's loop from his pocket and gave it a quick examination.

"It looks like a garnet," he said. "How amazing."

Each guest examined the strange stone, then returned it to their host.

While Dora excused herself to use the powder room, Sherman dropped the carbuncle into the red box and returned all three boxes to the shelf.

"You leave a priceless gem in a simple box?" Sam asked with a disapproving smirk. "With no security?"

Sherman puffed out his chest. "I am all the security it needs."

The guests stayed for another hour, then left at the same time. Normally, Sherman would have gone directly to bed. But some instinct led him back into the library.

He was shocked to see all three boxes lying open on the library table. Sherman went directly to the red box, then to the others. Sure enough, the carbuncle was gone.

He thought back. In the hour following the display of the jewel, each of his guests had wandered off, at least for a minute or two. It would have been chancy, but any one of them could have sneaked back into the library and stolen it.

Sherman was disappointed to think that one of his friends had robbed him. But his disappointment ran deeper. "Did the thief have such little regard for my detecting skills? How insulting! Would they have stolen from my great-great-grandfather and expected to get away with it?"

WHO STOLE THE BLUE CARBUNCLE?
WHAT GAVE THE THIEF AWAY?

Solution on page 89.

THE POKER FROM NOWHERE

Sherman Holmes and Sergeant Wilson stood side by side. They were staring at a bloody corpse sprawled face up in the living room of a suburban tract house.

Sherman spoke first. "A premeditated crime, what ho?"

Wilson frowned. "What makes you say that?"

"Choice of weapon." The round little man pointed at the fireplace poker. It had been used like a sword, stabbing its victim several times in the chest and stomach. "When we were walking up the drive, I didn't see any chimney."

Wilson looked around. "You're right. So, the killer brought the poker from another location, which indicates a planned murder. Very observant."

Holmes and Wilson had been in the midst of one of their occasional lunches when the call came in on the sergeant's cell phone. A mail carrier, making his rounds in a quiet neighborhood, had happened to glance through a living room window. He saw pretty much what they were seeing now, a large, elderly man who had died trying to fend off a brutal attack.

The responding patrolmen interviewed the next-door neighbor, a nearly deaf woman who claimed not to have heard or seen a thing.

"Harold Kipling." The sergeant was reading from the patrolman's notes. "A widower living alone. Three children, none of whom seemed fond of him. A life insurance policy was split among the kids, plus some savings. There had been fights about a nursing home and money."

"The children all live locally?" asked Sherman.

As if to answer the question, a patrolman eased open the door. "The victim's kids are here, Sarge. I told them he was dead. I hope that's okay."

The sergeant and his civilian partner walked out onto the lawn to face two middle-aged men and a woman. Wilson adopted his best corpse-side manner.

"Your father was murdered," he told them. "We don't know much more than that. The murder weapon was a fireplace poker."

"Fireplace poker? Dad doesn't have a fireplace," the older son said.

"We know that."

"So, what happened? Someone broke in with a poker and stabbed him to death?"

"There were no signs of forced entry," Wilson explained.

"Did your father get into many fights with people?"

The younger son found this amusing. "Just with us. He wanted to move into a nursing home. We didn't feel it was necessary."

"He wanted to go?" asked Wilson. This was certainly a switch.

"It's an expensive nursing home," volunteered the daughter. "He wanted to cash in his life insurance and use up his savings. It was a very selfish idea."

"I dropped over this morning," said Gary, the younger son. "Dad had already signed the papers. We argued about it, then I left. I called Jason and Jennifer."

"Right," said Jennifer. "Jason, Gary, and I decided we would come over as a group and try one last time. We got here just a few minutes ago."

"Can we see him?" Jason asked. There was a nervous timidity in his voice.

Sherman had been silent throughout the interview, but now he spoke up. "I think it would be fine for two of you to see the body. But one of you needs to answer a few more questions."

WHICH SUSPECT DOES SHERMAN WANT TO QUESTION?
WHAT CLUE MADE SHERMAN SUSPICIOUS?

Solution on page 89.

BIG DADDY BROWN

Sherman Holmes had been born and raised in Alabama and, despite his mania for Victorian England, had a deep, true affection for the American South. About once a year, usually on a warm spring weekend, he would gas up his antique Bentley and make the long pilgrimage back home.

Sherman himself was an orphan, but he had always kept in contact with his childhood neighbors, Big Daddy Brown and his clan. On one of his annual visits, the odd little detective found himself joining the Browns in every Alabamian's favorite pastime, a picnic.

The scene was a state park where the old southern family commandeered a picnic table. Big Daddy spread the tablecloth. Two of the grown children, Tiffany and Billy, unloaded the wicker baskets. The third, Julius, poured iced tea from a thermos, while Big Momma unpacked the crystal salt and pepper shakers and handed out cloth napkins. Sherman added his own touch, a candelabra topped with citronella candles to keep away the bugs.

Although he saw the Browns just once a year, Sherman felt he knew them intimately. Julius was close to his own age, while Tiffany and Billy, the twins, were a good ten years younger. None were married, as if forming a family of their own might be some sort of affront to the domineering father who controlled their lives.

On the surface, the picnic resembled the dozen previous

picnics he'd attended with the Browns. Billy flipped burg-
ers on the grill. Julius kept everyone's glass full. Tiffany
and Big Momma hovered over the proceedings, doling out
seconds and thirds, while Big Daddy slathered butter on his
corn, spilling half of it on his plate and wiping the other
half from his mouth with a napkin.

But something was wrong. The jokes were strained, the
affection too forced, and Sherman's sixth sense was kicking
into gear. He tried to ignore it.

Big Daddy's heart attack came suddenly, near the end of
the meal. The elderly man's fleshy face turned as white as
his neatly trimmed mustache. His breathing grew heavy.
Then he grasped his chest and collapsed backwards into the
grass.

Sherman and Julius rushed to Big Daddy's side. The others gathered around, looking on helplessly as the two men did their best to revive the stricken patriarch.

"He's dead," Julius whispered.

Tiffany ran off to call an ambulance, but everyone knew it would be too late.

"He's had heart problems before," Billy said, then turned to comfort his mother. "This was the best way to go, Momma, surrounded by family and eating his favorite food."

Sherman had seen a few heart attacks in his time, and this certainly looked like one. He'd also seen more than a few poisonings.

Sherman glanced over at Big Daddy's place at the table. His glass was half full of iced tea. His plate held the remains of potato salad, coleslaw, and the uneaten sliver of a hamburger bun. A clean but rumpled napkin sat beside the plate, right next to the crystal salt shaker.

The detective's heart sank. Why did people try to get away with murder when he was around? It just didn't make sense.

WHO KILLED BIG DADDY?
WHAT CLUE GAVE THE KILLER AWAY?

Solution on page 90.

THE RING-STEALING RING

The teenagers sat around the bare table in the small, bare room. All three chewed and snapped their gum and looked sullen. Sherman Holmes and Zach Alban, the jewelry store owner, stood by helplessly, watching the two boys and the girl as all of them continued to wait for the police.

Zach led Sherman out into the hall where they could talk privately. "Are you sure they stole the ring?" he asked with a nervous twitch.

Sherman sighed. He almost wished he hadn't gotten involved. He had walked into Alban Jewelers that morning to have his pocket watch fixed. Almost immediately, he became suspicious of the girl and her two friends hovering over the ring counter. As a matter of habit, Sherman made a quick perusal of the display case.

While Zach Alban was examining Sherman's century-old timepiece, the three teenagers started heading for the exit. Sherman threw another quick glance toward the ring counter. The centerpiece of the display, a sapphire and gold ring, was not where it had been just a minute before. It was gone.

For a short, heavyset person, Sherman could move surprisingly fast. "They're stealing a ring," he shouted as he raced to block the door.

The teenagers vehemently denied the theft and threatened a lawsuit if they weren't allowed to leave.

"I can't search them until the police arrive," Zach moaned. "Maybe it's all a mistake. Maybe I didn't put the ring out this morning. Or maybe someone stole it earlier and I didn't notice."

"The ring was there," Sherman assured him. "One of them stole it."

Red and white lights flashed through the windows as a police cruiser pulled into the handicap parking space. Two officers entered, were briefed on the situation, and were led into the small back room.

The female officer searched the girl, Hanna Bright, while the male officer frisked both Josh Ingram and Timmy Bright, Hanna's brother. Their possessions were searched as well. A quick visual inspection of the room showed no place where the ring could have been hidden.

Zach Alban was profuse with apologies to everyone except Sherman. When the teens complained of being hungry, Zach ran out to the fast-food restaurant next door and returned a few minutes later with mounds of food. Hanna and Josh removed the wads of gum from their mouths before sinking into the hot double cheeseburgers.

"We came in to buy a present for Josh's mom." Food was sticking to Hanna's braces as she spoke. "Is this how you treat customers? We're telling everyone not to shop here."

"Maybe we'll organize a boycott," Josh added. "How would you like a picket line, Mr. Alban?"

Sherman took Zach aside. "I wasn't wrong," he insisted. "One of those kids took the ring. And what's more, I can prove it."

WHO STOLE THE RING?
WHERE IS THE RING NOW?

Solution on page 91.

MRS. KRENSHAW'S
SPARE KEY

"I hate to bother you, Mr. Holmes."

Sherman's neighbor, Mrs. Krenshaw, led him across the street from his house to hers, a tidy Victorian gem set in the pristine white of a recent snowfall. The elderly widow was remarkably self-sufficient and walked with a strong, confident gait.

"I know I ought to go to the police," she said in a fluttering voice. "But Hank and Edgar are both such good friends. If you could find some way of getting my vase back without calling in the authorities..." She pressed her hand into his. "You're so very clever about these things."

Sherman blushed and cleared his throat. "Tell me about the vase, Mrs. Krenshaw."

She spoke eagerly. "You know that TV program, *America's Treasures*, the one where people bring in antiques and the experts tell where they came from and how much they're worth. Well, I had this old vase handed down to me by my mother. I took it over to the Armory yesterday, where they were filming the show. An expert appraised it at $20,000. It was all very exciting, being on TV and having such a rarity."

"And you think either Hank or Edgar broke into your house and stole it?"

"I don't know what else to think. Look."

Sherman looked. In the middle of the lawn sat a flower-pot on top of a stump. A single set of footprints crossed the snow-covered lawn to the stump then crossed away again toward the front door. Mrs. Krenshaw trampled through the snow to the stump.

"The house was unlocked when I got home from shopping a few minutes ago. I never leave it unlocked. Sure enough, the antique vase was gone. Then I saw these footprints out here. I came right over to you." She lifted the flowerpot and pointed to a key hidden beneath it. "I know it's stupid to leave a key out here like this, but everybody does it."

"Both Edgar and Hank know where you keep your spare key?"

"Yes. And they knew about the vase. I just had to tell them my wonderful news."

Once inside the house, Sherman telephoned Hank, Lyda Krenshaw's next-door neighbor, and Edgar, a gentleman friend who lived two blocks away. Hank was the first to arrive.

"I've been home all morning," Hank explained. He was a young, slight bachelor and didn't seem outraged to be considered a suspect. "I was paying bills at my desk. It's got a view of the street and I didn't notice any cars stopping or people walking by. Of course, I wasn't staring out the window every second." Sherman checked the man's shoes. They were wet from the snow, but his trouser legs appeared dry.

Edgar rang the bell a few minutes later. He seemed more annoyed by Sherman's inquiries. "I took my dog for a walk this morning. I passed by this block, but I didn't see anyone. And I certainly didn't go into Lyda's house."

Sherman left the men and joined Mrs. Krenshaw in the kitchen. "I'm not sure I can help you," he admitted. "Was the vase insured?"

She thought for a moment. "I suppose it's covered by my homeowner's policy. Does this mean you don't know who took it?"

"Oh, I know who took it. I just don't think you'll like the answer."

WHO STOLE THE VASE?
WHAT CLUE GAVE THE THIEF AWAY?

Solution on page 92.

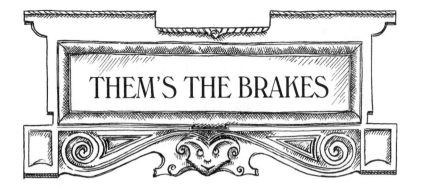

THEM'S THE BRAKES

It was a balmy, late summer evening. Sergeant Wilson examined the mangled body in the driver's seat, exchanging a few words with his forensics crew. When he finally trudged up the side of the ravine to the break in the railing, he was only slightly surprised to find Sherman Holmes pulling his antique Bentley into the roadside turnout.

"Well, that clinches it," Wilson muttered. "If Sherman shows up on the scene, it's got to be murder. Good evening, Mr. Holmes."

"Evening, my good Wilson." Sherman scanned the broken railing and the winding, downhill road leading to it. "No tire marks. May we assume that the driver's brakes malfunctioned?"

"Brake lines were neatly cut. The victim is one Milton Graves. His driver's license says he lives up the hill. Want to join me while I break the news to his next of kin?"

The men hopped into a police cruiser and hopped out again in front of a comfortable mountain retreat. The thirtyish, attractive woman answering the door identified herself as Dominique Black, the niece and personal lawyer of the deceased.

Dominique seemed stunned by the tragic news and asked the sergeant and his companion to step inside. The first thing Sherman noticed was a balloon bouquet nestled high in the oaken rafters.

"A birthday party?" he inquired.

"For Uncle Milton," she answered. "My cousins and I came over for a little celebration. Afterwards, Uncle Milton drove off to pick up another cousin at the airport. We were expecting them back any moment. And now you say he's dead?"

"Yes, ma'am. Probably just minutes after leaving the house." Wilson didn't mention the brake lines.

The other inhabitants wandered into the entry hall and were informed of the news. The cousins, Tyrone and Chuck Graves, seemed just as stunned as Dominique, while the housekeeper, Mrs. Watts, reacted with a chilly frown.

"Do you know anyone who might have wanted your uncle dead?"

"I can think of three," Mrs. Watts answered. "During dessert, Mr. Graves made an announcement. He had just changed his will. Instead of leaving his money to charity, he had divided his estate evenly among his nieces and nephews."

"That's right," Tyrone admitted. "It came as a complete shock."

"What a tragic coincidence!" Chuck could barely repress a grin.

"Exactly," agreed Sherman. "What did you all do after dinner?"

Chuck, a Wall Street broker, answered first. "I was overwhelmed by the news. I telephoned my wife as soon as we left the table. I was still on the phone when Uncle Milton drove off."

Tyrone, a pediatric surgeon, had a similar, equally provable alibi. "I was on my cell phone, talking to the hospital. I imagine the phone company can verify the time."

"And I was with Uncle Milton," Dominique said, "taping a video birthday greeting for the company offices. Mrs. Watts was working the camera."

Mrs. Watts nodded. "Why do you need to know this, officer?"

"For our report," Wilson replied, then took Sherman aside. He looked disappointed. "If their stories check out, Sherman, we're stumped. None of them had a chance to get to the garage and tamper with the brakes."

"But someone did tamper with the brakes," Sherman said. "And I think I know who."

WHO CUT THE BRAKE LINES?
HOW DID SHERMAN KNOW?

Solution on page 92.

DEATH OF A SWINGER

"We had an abandoned quarry like this back home." Despite the tragic scene, Sherman couldn't repress a smile. "The local swimming hole. I remember being a kid and swinging on a rope, Tarzan-style, just like this poor fellow."

His wistful tone contrasted sharply with the bloody, broken body just in front of him. The deceased was a youth of about twenty, wearing swim trunks and lying on a granite slab a dozen feet from the edge of a deep, clear pool. Wreathing the body was a thirty-foot length of rope.

Sergeant Wilson lifted the corpse to reveal the rope's freshly severed end. "See? The rope was cut halfway through, then torn the rest of the way." He held the body

up as Sherman inspected the rope, then settled the body back down on top of it. "This was murder."

Both men turned and looked up the sheer rock face. Sixty feet above them was the cliff on which Bobby Fixx had stood. Even from here, Sherman could see the other end of the rope, tied to the branch of a towering pine. The ten-foot section swayed gently in the summer breeze.

"Looks pretty obvious," Wilson said. "Our Mr. Fixx swings out on the rope, just like he's done a hundred times before. Only this time, someone's cut through it. Instead of swinging into the water, he falls straight down, taking this useless piece of rope with him."

"Isn't this area private property?" asked Sherman.

"Yep," said Wilson. "Owned by Midlands Granite. Fixx and his college buddies rent an off-campus house just over the ridge. Let's go pay them a visit."

They found the three college juniors sitting in stunned silence on the porch of a tattered cabin. Sergeant Wilson checked his notes. "Thad Killian? You actually saw it happen?"

"Yeah." The short blond boy on the porch swing nodded his head. "I was hiking along the ridge, a couple hundred yards from the cliff. I saw Bobby. He grabbed the rope and took a running start. As soon as he cleared the edge, the rope broke. He screamed and then there was this thud instead of a splash. I came right back here and called 911."

"I heard the scream, too," said a tall, burly redhead. "I'm Rick Dawson. I was walking on the road, by the barbed-wire fence. I figured the scream must have come from the swimming quarry. That's the only reason anyone goes there. I hopped the fence and found his body a few minutes later. I didn't touch anything."

"Forensics will know if you did," the sergeant said curtly. He approached the third student. "You must be Julio Mendez."

"Right," answered the last roommate. "I was supposed to go swimming with Bobby today, but I fell asleep. Thad woke me after he called 911." He shivered. "I used that rope swing as much as Bobby. It could have been me dying like that."

Wilson took his friend aside. "This could be a hard one, Sherman. We don't even know if Fixx was the intended target. Whoever sawed through that rope..."

"Whoever sawed through that rope is right here on this porch. I don't know what the motive was, but one of Fixx's roommates is definitely lying."

WHO KILLED BOBBY FIXX?
WHAT GAVE THE KILLER AWAY?

Solution on page 93.

THE MISSING LINK

"This is a first," Wilson said with a bemused smile. "A guy with a bathroom in his office."

"This new office came with Mr. Seaver's recent promotion," explained Lisa, the dead man's secretary. She was young and tall and solidly built, in a modest skirt and blouse. "The workmen just finished putting in the bathroom over the weekend."

"I wonder if he ever got to use it?" Sherman mused. "Other than to die in, I mean."

It was Monday morning. Sherman and the sergeant were on the eighteenth floor of the Krall Building, in the private bathroom of the private office of Archie Seaver, newly appointed president of Krall Electronics. Seaver, a large, thin man, lay on the floor, strangled from behind, presumably with the necktie lying beside him. He was dressed for work, although his suit jacket was hung on a hook and his white shirt was unbuttoned and untucked.

"Why would a man who just arrived at work have his shirt half off?" Sherman muttered to himself.

"What are you looking for?" asked Wilson.

Sherman was bent over, inspecting the floor. "The other cufflink." It was only then that Wilson noticed it. The deceased was wearing one gold cufflink, while the other cuff spilled open over his other hand.

"There it is." Wilson donned a pair of plastic gloves, then

tried to reach behind the toilet where the cufflink was tightly lodged. There was no way he could reach it.

"Forensics will find a way to get it," he said with a shrug, then turned to Lisa. "You discovered the body, Miss?"

Lisa nodded. "Mr. Seaver was always the first one in, usually around 7:30. I got in at 8:15. I put on a pot of coffee and then came straight here. I screamed and the others came running."

"Others?"

It seemed that two other Krall employees had been on the eighteenth floor at the time. Lisa escorted Sergeant Wilson and Holmes to their offices.

Brian McKay, a large, jovial man, was the company's executive vice president. "I got in at eight," he told the investigators. "My office is on the other side. I was just catching up on my E-mail when I heard Lisa screaming."

"Were you a candidate for Seaver's job?" Wilson asked darkly.

McKay just laughed. "You don't have to go that far to find a motive. Archie Seaver was an abusive opportunist. Lots of people probably wanted to strangle him."

Ed Washington, the third suspect, was short and slight, but seemed to have a more violent nature than the others. "I got here a minute before Brian," he said with begrudging civility. "I popped my head in Archie's door and we chatted about some new deadlines. Then I went around to my office and closed the door. I didn't hear a thing until Lisa called out."

Sherman couldn't help noticing that both Washington and McKay were in their shirtsleeves, tie-less and with their collars unbuttoned.

Sergeant Wilson finished his last interview, and then turned to find Sherman gone. He found his friend kneeling in Seaver's brand-new bathroom, buttoning the top button of the victim's shirt. "A loose fit," he murmured.

"What are you doing?" bellowed Wilson.

"Solving the case," Sherman said as he got to his feet and brushed off his knees.

WHO KILLED ARCHIE SEAVER?
WHAT CLUE GAVE THE KILLER AWAY?

Solution on page 94.

THE TAUNTING CLUE

Sherman felt honored. He'd had no idea the police commissioner even knew he existed. And now, not only was he at headquarters actually meeting the head man, but Commissioner Lowry was asking him for advice.

"Sergeant Wilson says you've helped him on one or two cases. Perhaps you can give us a fresh viewpoint on this one."

"I'll try," Sherman said, doing his best to look modest.

"Good." Lowry consulted the notes on his desk. "Yesterday at three P.M., a jogger on County Lane Road heard a gunshot. He pulled out his cell phone and called 911. A few minutes later, a patrol car made a pass through the area and found a murder victim, Andy Patano, a mobster we were leaning on to get information on some bigger fish. He'd been shot in the head, execution-style. Under the body, our boys found a cigarette lighter — gold, with the initials B.F."

Sherman didn't have to think hard. "The mob boss, Bruno Friendly."

"Exactly. And Bruno's prints were on the lighter. We finally thought we had the mob boss dead to rights, except for one thing."

"Bruno has an alibi for three P.M.?"

Lowry nodded. "From two P.M. to three. Bruno is always alone at that hour, taking an afternoon nap. A pair of my detectives had decided that would be a good time to pay him a visit and put on some pressure about his gambling operations. They were with him at his house when Patano was killed."

Sherman appreciated the irony. "So, the police graciously supplied Bruno with an ironclad alibi. How did Bruno explain his cigarette lighter being under the victim?"

"Bruno says he used the lighter that morning during a breakfast meeting with his three lieutenants. When my detectives were there, Bruno made a point of not being able to find it. We're being played for fools, Sherman, and I don't like it."

"What about Bruno's lieutenants? Could one of them have committed the murder?"

Commissioner Lowry checked his notes. "None of them has an alibi. Max A. was at Bruno's house when the detectives arrived. From there, he says he went to the market, paid cash for some groceries, then went straight home.

"Joey B. telephoned Bruno shortly after 2:30, while my men were there. Bruno mentioned he had unexpected guests but didn't elaborate. Joey was calling from his cell phone, so he could have been anywhere. He says he was at his mother's house, baking a pan of ziti."

"And the third guy?"

"That's Carl C. He says he was at a matinee movie from two to four. He has a ticket stub and knows the movie's plot, but that's no real alibi." Lowry slammed a fist on his desk. "This thing with Bruno's lighter. It's like they're playing with us, telling us they did it and daring us to catch them."

Sherman scratched his chin. "If you do put Bruno in jail, will that shut down his operation?"

"I wish," grumbled Lowry. "No. There'll be a power vacuum. But in a few weeks, one of Bruno's lieutenants will wind up taking his place."

"Well, I think we can prevent that from happening."

Lowry seemed confused by the comment, then his eyes widened. "What are you saying? You have the murder solved?"

"Oh, yes. Looking at it from the outside makes it fairly easy."

WHO KILLED ANDY PATANO?
WHAT CLUE DID SHERMAN LATCH ONTO?

Solution on page 95.

SOLUTIONS

The Missing Monet

"All three suspects had receptacles that could hold a rolled-up painting." Sherman was doing his best to make his Alabama-born accent sound British. "The messenger had a document tube, old boy. The uncle had a cane. The woman had an umbrella. And while it's tempting to accuse the last person to walk through the reception area, that wouldn't be cricket. The painting could have been cut out of its frame at any time and no one may have noticed."

Wilson snickered. "So it could be any of them."

"And it could be an employee who found someplace clever to hide the painting. But only one suspect arrived limping on one leg and departed limping on the other. I think if you examine the older gentleman's cane you'll find that it's hollow."

"You may be right," the sergeant said. "We'll check it out. But let me fill you in on something, old boy. You're no relation to Sherlock Holmes. Sherlock Holmes was fictional."

Sherman laughed. "Nonsense. Why would Dr. Watson make up those stories if they weren't true?"

"Because Dr. Watson was also fict...Oh, forget it."

A Maze of Suspects

The audience of five squirmed in the narrow corner of the hedge until they were all facing the strange little man with the funny accent. "Two of your stories agree on one point. The electricity was turned off — from shortly after Mr. and Mrs. Turner's arrival until after the murder."

The highway patrolman laughed. "It doesn't take a Sherlock Holmes to figure that out."

"Sherman Holmes," the little man corrected the patrolman. "And as I said, the solution is elementary. Since the fountain in the center of the maze works by electricity, it couldn't have been running at the time of the murder, as Mr. McQuire testified. Of course, Mr. McQuire didn't know the fountain was off, because he was somewhere else at the time — robbing and killing Kyle Turner, I presume."

Bus Station Bomber

The two cab drivers, the clerk, and the bomb squad officer all gaped in disbelief.

Sergeant Wilson tried to look nonchalant. "I caught the clue, too," he lied. "But I'll let you have the fun of telling them."

"Thanks," Sherman said, playing along. "If the perpetrator had picked a more complex bomb, it wouldn't have been so easy."

"But that's what makes it hard," the bomb squad officer objected. "You can buy a wind-up clock just about anywhere. And as for the sticks of dynamite..."

"Let's stick with the clock," interrupted Sherman. "The alarm hand is what set off the explosives, correct?"

"Correct."

"So, let's say it's two A.M. and I set the alarm for three. When will the bomb go off? At three A.M. — or at three P.M. the next day?"

"At three A.M., of course, an hour later."

"Then how do you explain the fact that the bomb didn't go off until thirteen hours after the witness saw it placed inside the locker?"

The bomb expert scratched his head. "I can't explain it."

"That's right," Sherman said. "There's no way to explain it, except to say that the night clerk is lying. He planted the bomb himself — at some time after three A.M."

The Postman Rings Once

"If it wasn't suicide," said Thomas, "then any one of us could have killed him. No one has a good alibi."

"True," Wilson agreed and turned to Sherman Holmes.

"True," Sherman agreed. "But..." And he raised a pudgy finger. "Only one of you lied about when you checked the mail." He lowered the finger, pointing it at Nigel Liggit. "You, Nigel, actually entered the front hall between 2:30 and 2:50. You steamed open the letter and read its frightening contents. You got rid of the letter — a bad job, I must say — then loaded your uncle's gun and tracked him down."

"Bravo," Nigel said with a sneer. "But you could make up a similar story about either one of my brothers."

Sherman smiled. "Let's see Thomas's letter from that bill collector." Thomas pulled it from his pocket and handed it over. "Notice the shoe print?"

"That's mine," said Gerald, "from when I came in and stepped on the mail."

"And the water ring? Where did that come from?"

"Not from me," said Thomas. "My hands were full of luggage. I went right upstairs and unpacked."

Sherman turned to face Nigel and his incriminating martini. "When you checked the mail, you put your glass on top of Thomas's letter. That means you didn't check it at three p.m., but earlier — between the time of Gerald's shoe print and Thomas's removal of the bill collector's letter."

Foul Ball Burglary

"Excuse me," a high-pitched voice drawled. "I can tell you who stole the coins — if you're interested."

The startled officers turned to see a dapper little man step out from behind the leafy palm fronds. "Who are you?" the tall one demanded.

"Sherman Holmes, at your service. The thief was Jake."

"Jake?" The tall officer had to think for a second. "You mean the kid who discovered the robbery? How could he be the robber?"

Sherman knew he had their attention. He took his time, reaching into his coat pocket and pulling out a briar pipe.

"What young Jake discovered," Sherman said as he sucked on the unlit pipe, "was a broken window, a screeching burglar alarm, and a coin collection lying temptingly on the table. All he had to do was yell back that there'd been a robbery. Then, while the rest of us went around to the front of the house, Jake slipped inside, turned over the table, and took the coins. They may be in his pockets or he may have hidden them somewhere. But Jake's your thief."

The tall officer still looked interested. "Can you prove what you just said?"

"Of course, old bean," Sherman said, insulted at the notion that he would form a theory without proof. "Go back to the crime scene and check the broken window glass. It's underneath the tablecloth. That means the table was over-turned after the baseball broke the window, not before. It couldn't be anyone but Jake."

The Unsafe Safe House

"The name is Sherman Holmes, private investigator." He took a deep breath then turned to the rookie. "Please arrest Captain Loeb."

"What?" Loeb was instantly furious. "That's garbage. I'll have your P.I. license revoked so fast..."

For once Sherman was glad he didn't have a license. "Ask the captain how he could have arrived without a coat and yet was planning to leave with one. And don't let him say it's not his coat. His notepad was in the pocket."

The rookie's hand shook as he pulled his service revolver. "Are you sure, mister?"

"I am," Sherman replied. "I've been staring at that bloody trench coat for an hour. Frankie would naturally open the door to the captain in charge of his case. Loeb took off his coat, made himself comfortable, then strangled Frankie with his belt. It was only after leaving the house, with the front door locked behind him, that the captain realized he'd left his coat inside."

The Crystal Vanishes

"The crystal didn't abandon you," Sherman said. "It's just playing a little joke." He had to handle this delicately. The last thing he wanted was to put an end to these weekly events, something that would surely happen if one of his spirit-loving friends were exposed as a thief.

"If memory serves, Luther freshened our coffee just a few minutes ago. And yet the coffee carafe still seems to be full." Sherman carried the glass carafe into the kitchen and carefully emptied the contents into the sink. Sitting there in the bottom of the carafe was the crystal ball. "You see? It dematerialized from the box and rematerialized here."

Agatha and Grimelda laughed with relief. So did Luther, although Sherman caught his eye and gave him a serious, warning glance, letting Luther know that he knew the truth. While clearing the table, Luther had sneaked the crystal out of the box and into the carafe. As the host, he could have easily recovered it after the others had left.

The Pointing Corpse

Sergeant Wilson scratched his head. "There's no way you can know what he was pointing at."

"Oh, yes, there is," Sherman said. "His battery's dead."

"So what?"

"So, a dead battery probably means his lights were on." Sherman checked the dashboard and saw that he was right. "Let's say Mervin had a rendezvous here last night with someone from the Charity Board, perhaps to get information for his story. That person realized Mervin was getting too close to the truth and killed him. But before dying, Mervin saw something..."

"Yeah, yeah," Wilson growled. "And he pointed to it. But which of the three things was he pointing at?"

"It was night, remember? The lake and trees would have been invisible in the dark, especially with all the cloud cover we've had lately. The one visible thing would have been that glowing neon sign. That's what Mervin meant. The killer was Arthur Curtis."

Bell, Booke, or Kendal?

"It was the intern," Wilson guessed.

Sherman looked surprised. "No, of course not. There was no thief."

"Sure there was. Mr. Boren told us..." The sergeant's eyes widened. "Oh!"

"Precisely. I don't know why Arvin Boren wanted to kill his vice president, but it had nothing to do with stolen plans. He killed Silver in the copy room, then he found a witness and 'discovered' the body. Boren made up that story about Silver trying to catch the thief and, of course, Silver wasn't around to contradict him."

"What made you suspect Boren?"

"I suspected from the beginning, but I had no proof. So I made up a story about the plans having to be in the mail chute. Boren needed to preserve the illusion of a thief, so he grabbed a set of plans and tossed them down the chute. That's the only way to explain why the plans are on top of the yellow envelopes instead of underneath them."

The Wayward Will

Sherman edged his considerable bulk between Harmon Grove and the briefcase. Then, like a quarterback, he tucked the leather briefcase under his arm and lurched around to the far side of the table. "The will is in here."

"You're crazy," Harmon shouted. "Don't open that. It's private."

Sherman was already rummaging through the miscellaneous files and papers. "Ah, what do you know! Here it is!" And with a flourish, Sherman pulled out the signed document.

"I don't know why Jacob cut you out of his will, Harmon, old man. Had he lived another week, he might have put you back in. It must have seemed very arbitrary and unjust. So, you just pretended the will was missing."

Anna's mouth was agape. "How do you know that?"

"Harmon said he was in the new will, but that couldn't

be true. Harmon, you see, signed as a witness. And, as he himself told me, you can't witness a will in which you inherit."

The Doc's Last Lunch

Sherman went to the doctor's refrigerator and opened the freezer section. "No ice in the ice tray. Just as I suspected. That's how the doctor's last patient got the kettle not to whistle until 12:35. He filled it with ice cubes and put it on a low flame."

"You mean the killer was the patient I saw leaving?"

"Yes. This nut case, as Ms. Gould so aptly put it, was clever enough to make the crime appear to have happened later. He rigged the kettle, opened the tuna, and sliced the apple. He probably even moved the body into the kitchen."

"That's a cute theory," Wilson said. "But..."

"Note the oxidated flesh of the apple." Sherman pointed to the browned fruit, then to the fruit knife in the victim's hand. "If the doctor had cut the apple himself, as we're meant to believe, it couldn't have turned so brown so soon. We discovered the body just minutes after he supposedly cut it."

A Halloween Homicide

"The accident was definitely staged," Sherman whispered to his friend. "Someone came in the back way, probably bringing the mask and candy, too. Miss Cleghorn was pushed down the stairs and the scene was set. You were meant to come to the exact conclusion you came to."

"Get off it," Wilson growled. "Every death isn't a murder."

"Those pearls at the top of the stairs? You try slipping on

them and see if they stay in place. In a real accident, the string would break. At the very least, the pearls would have slid out from under her feet."

"Oh." Wilson took a deep breath. "I see your point."

"If I were you, I'd question Emma. We never mentioned that Miss Wilson had fallen down the stairs, and yet she instantly assumed it."

A Commercial Break Break-In

"You don't have to get snippy," Sherman said. His feelings were hurt, but not enough to keep him from showing off. "First off, this was an inside job. When Trent stepped on the ladder, it crunched through the snow, proving that it had never supported any weight."

Amelia Warner gasped. "You're saying it was one of us? Let me tell you, Mr. Sherman Holmes..."

Sherman scurried behind Trent, as if looking for protection. And then, in a split second, he pulled the revolver from the guard's holster.

Sherman trained the gun on the startled guard. "It couldn't have been someone from inside the house because there were no snowy footprints leading to the door. So whoever put up the ladder didn't come out of the house or go back into it. If you'll check Mr. Trent's coat pockets, I believe you'll find the jewelry and cash."

"Me?" Trent bristled. "I'm the one who discovered the ladder."

"After you planted it there. While we thought you were so bravely searching the upstairs rooms, you were actually robbing them."

An Alarming Jewel Heist

"The alarm didn't catch anyone." Zach still sounded angry.

"Yes, it did. Tell me, Zach. How long do you think the thief took to clean you out?"

Zach glanced around the showroom. "A minimum of five minutes, probably ten."

"And yet, when the police got here two minutes after the alarm, the burglar was already gone."

"Yeah." Zach scratched his head. "That's impossible."

"Not if the burglar was already inside. After we left, he came out of hiding and took what he wanted. He set off the alarm when he left the shop, not when he arrived."

"You say he. It was a man?"

"It was Sam Wells. He was the only person we didn't actually see exiting the shop. He must have hidden in a closet or behind a counter until after we left. It had to be him. No one else could have come in while we were still here, not without setting off the door buzzer."

All in the Family

"George Gleason didn't have a chance to ask any questions," Wilson explained confidently. "He saw the victim's bloody head and the rifle and assumed Lovett had been shot. But, of course, he hadn't been."

"And that indicates his innocence?"

"Absolutely. He's protecting his kids."

"Which is exactly what he wants us to think."

Wilson frowned. "What are you talking about?"

"Gleason wants us to think he's making a false confession. He knew we'd pick up on his mistake and strike him off our suspect list. Very clever of him."

"How do you figure that?"

"Because he knew Lovett had been killed last night. Lovett is often here early, but he rarely stays past noon. An innocent man would have assumed Lovett had been killed this morning. Only the person who telephoned him last night and lured him here would know when Lovett had been ambushed and killed."

The Lost Etruscan Find

"I don't believe you," Sergeant Wilson growled. "You know who did it."

It pained Sherman to lie, but he managed to swallow his pride. "On the contrary, Wilson. I'm completely stumped."

Wilson bellowed, but Sherman stuck to his story.

After Wilson and the others left, Professor Plotny breathed a sigh of relief. "Thank you, old friend, for not giving me away."

"Well, you didn't commit any crime, other than breaking a school skylight. The statuette was a forgery, I imagine?"

"Right," the professor admitted. "I didn't discover it until yesterday with Westbank. Luckily, he was new to the piece and too jet-lagged to see it. A clever forgery, but one that could ruin my reputation. I had to get rid of it or else be made a laughingstock. What gave me away?"

Sherman pointed to the floor. "The rainwater. It means the skylight was broken before the rain stopped at seven last night. But according to your story, you didn't leave the library until 7:15."

Plotny nodded. "I used the ladder to get up the skylight and fake the break-in. The rain was just beginning to let up. I never thought it might give me away."

Blue Carbuncle, the Sequel

Sherman would have loved to do a full crime scene examination, but it really wasn't necessary. As soon as he'd discovered his loss, he knew the most probable suspect.

He checked his address book, got into his car, and drove to Dora Treat's house, arriving just minutes after the nurse practitioner herself.

"You did it as a challenge," he said as she answered the door. "I know you wouldn't really steal from me."

Dora looked confused for a second. "How did you know..." A variety of emotions seemed to cross her face. The last one looked a lot like resignation. "Yes, of course, a challenge. I thought it might be nice to have another 'Adventure of the Blue Carbuncle.'"

"Oh, I knew it had to be a joke," Sherman said with obvious relief.

"Of course." Reaching into her purse, she returned the small, blue gemstone. "What gave me away?"

"You were in a hurry, correct? Any second and I might have walked in and caught you. And yet you searched through all three boxes."

"And that eliminated the others?"

"Both Sam and Buddy saw me put the carbuncle in the red box. But you weren't in the room at the time. You were the only one who didn't know which box held the carbuncle."

The Poker from Nowhere

The patrolman ushered the daughter and the younger son into the house, while Sherman stood on the brick path and smiled benignly at the victim's oldest child.

"Does your house have a fireplace, Jason?"

"As a matter of fact, it doesn't. But Jennifer's got one. And I think there's one in Gary's apartment."

"Is that why you chose a poker as the murder weapon? We can trace where you bought it, you know."

"What are you talking about?" Jason's voice rose in anger. "Are you accusing me of stabbing my father?"

"I am. How do you know he was stabbed?"

Jason stopped and looked confused. "The poker. You said he was killed with a poker."

"That's right. And if I told a dozen people that a man had been killed with a poker, I expect the full dozen would assume he'd been hit — bludgeoned, if you will. It's by far the easier, more common way to use the instrument. And yet, you somehow knew he'd been stabbed."

Big Daddy Brown

"I don't want to turn you in," Sherman said softly.

It was two days later and the family was walking away from the burial site, heading back to the funeral home's limousine parked by the cemetery's gravel road.

Sherman had maneuvered his way to Big Momma's side. They were out of earshot of the others and would be for the next minute or two.

"I don't want to turn you in," he repeated. "Why did you do it?"

"For the kids," said Big Momma. Her tone was eerily calm. "You saw how it was. All the time he pushed them down, controlled everything. Maybe now they can live their own lives. Me, too," she added as an afterthought.

"You poisoned his napkin." Sherman had to show her that he knew. "Every time he went to wipe his mouth, he inhaled a little poison. Then after he collapsed and no one was looking, you replaced it with a clean napkin. That's what I noticed. A clean napkin — that should have been covered with butter."

"You can't prove it," Big Momma said with a thin smile. "Even if you dig up the body and check it for poison, that napkin no longer exists. You can't prove a thing."

The Ring-Stealing Ring

Zach eyed his old friend with evident distrust. "Sherman, if you can prove they stole the ring, why didn't you do it ten minutes ago?"

"I would have proved it earlier, but legally we couldn't search them."

"Search them?" Zach was livid. "What are you talking about? The police just did search them."

Sherman was used to holding his temper and being polite. "Before you and I left the back room," he said calmly, "all three suspects were chewing gum, correct?"

Zach thought for a second. "Correct."

"And yet, when it came time to eat the hamburgers, only two of them removed the gum from their mouths. What happened to the third kid's gum?"

"I don't know. Maybe he swallowed it."

Without another word of speculation, Sherman walked into the back room. Kneeling down, he checked under the table and the chairs. "Here it is," he said, lifting up a chair and showing the underside. "Timmy's chair. I'm also willing to bet this is Timmy's gum stuck on the bottom and your ring stuck in the middle of it. I won't touch it, in case there's a partial print."

Mrs. Krenshaw's Spare Key

Mrs. Krenshaw was confused. "Of course I won't like the answer, Mr. Holmes. It's never nice to find out someone is a thief."

"Well, on that score you don't have to worry. Neither Hank nor Edgar stole the vase. You did."

"Me?"

Sherman nodded. "I assume you did this as a dry run, to see if your little scheme would pass muster when you tell it to the police. It won't, dear lady."

"What do you mean? Why would I steal my own vase?"

"For the insurance money. Since the vase was just appraised by an expert, your homeowner's insurance would have to pay."

The elderly woman scowled. "All right. Where did I screw up? Did you see me from your window?"

"No. Those footprints in the snow gave you away."

"How? I wore a pair of my late husband's shoes."

"But there was only one set. If the thief took the key, unlocked the door, and later returned the key to the flower-pot, then there would have been two sets of prints, one when he took the key and one when he returned it. The thief — you — made those prints to throw suspicion on someone else. Then you used your own key to get in and out."

Them's the Brakes

"You can't know who it is." Given Sherman's record, Sergeant Wilson hated to disagree, but this was one time when he saw no possible explanation. "Are you saying their alibis won't check out?"

"Not at all," said Sherman. "They might indeed. Chuck might well have been on the phone the entire time. The same might be true for Tyrone. As for Dominique, if we didn't believe Mrs. Watts's testimony, then we could check the time stamp on the video recorder. I assume that they're all telling the truth."

"Well, then, when were the brake lines cut?"

Sherman paused for effect. "Before dinner, old boy."

"Before...?" Wilson had to smile. "You're slipping, old boy. Mr. Graves only announced his will at the dinner table. Before dinner, no one had a reason to want him dead."

Now it was Sherman's time to smile. "If you were Graves and you were changing your will, who would you go to?"

"A lawyer, of course."

"And who was Milton Graves's lawyer? His niece, Dominique."

"You're right." Wilson slapped his leg. "We'll check that will. If Dominique drew it up, then she goes to the top of our list — the only suspect who knew ahead of time about the inheritance."

Death of a Swinger

"Did you fellows all get along?" Sherman asked in his most innocuous tone. "Was Bobby a good friend?"

The roommates exchanged glances. "Well..." Julio hemmed. "Bobby had this habit of stealing girls. He never messed with my Angie, but I heard from other guys. He got this perverse pleasure from going after girls who were already dating."

"I doubt that was true," said Thad Killian. "Just gossip, you know."

"Then why did you kill him?" asked Sherman.

Thad chuckled. "What do you mean?"

"You killed him, Thad. You cut the rope and threw it off the cliff. Then, when Bobby showed up to swim, you pushed him off the cliff."

Thad stopped chuckling. "That's ridiculous."

"Your story was ridiculous. Bobby didn't swing on that rope as you said. If he had, the severed rope end would have landed on top of his body or beside it. But the rope end was found underneath him. He couldn't have been swinging on it when he fell."

The Missing Link

Wilson was still angry. "You know better than to touch the victim at a crime scene."

"I know," Sherman said by way of apology. "But I had to make sure that the collar didn't fit."

Wilson looked confused. "You knew it would be too big?"

"I suspected the victim wasn't wearing his own shirt, yes. That's the easiest way of explaining why it was unbuttoned and untucked."

Wilson paused and thought, but it still didn't make sense. "Perhaps you should explain a bit more."

Sherman beamed. "Elementary, my dear friend. Let's say I'm the killer. I sneak up behind my victim in his bathroom and strangle him with a tie. My tie or his tie, we don't really know."

"Forget about the ties," growled Wilson.

"During the act of murder, one of my cufflinks gets loose and falls behind the toilet where I can't retrieve it. So what do I do?"

Wilson thought some more. "Maybe you change cufflinks with the victim, so the police think it's the victim's cufflink behind the toilet."

"And if the victim isn't wearing a shirt that accommodates cufflinks?"

"Then maybe you change shirts with the victim."

"Exactly. That explains why the shirt is unbuttoned and untucked. And it explains why the collar is too loose. Remember our large friend, Brian McKay? Check the shirt he's wearing, I believe you'll find that his collar is too tight."

The Taunting Clue

Police Commissioner Lowry pushed himself to his feet. "I knew you could do it. Who was it? And what did you mean about looking at it from the outside?"

Sherman tried to be diplomatic. "I mean leaving out the pride and the embarrassment and the idea of their taunting you. No one was taunting anybody."

"Are you sure?"

"Positive. Bruno didn't know ahead of time that your detectives were coming. From two to three was his nap time. Normally he wouldn't have an alibi at all. It was just luck that he did."

"So, what are you saying? One of Bruno's own lieutenants was trying to frame Bruno for murder?"

"Exactly. They were the only three who could have taken the lighter from his house that morning. One of them killed Patano, planted the lighter, and hoped to take over the boss's position when the boss got sent to jail."

"Nice theory," Lowry said with a nod. "But that still leaves us with three suspects."

"No, just one, Carl C. The other two both knew about Bruno's unexpected visitors. If either of them were planning the murder, he would have postponed it to another day. Carl was the only one who had access to the lighter and who didn't know that Bruno would have an alibi."

INDEX